Michael Rosen

OFF THE WALL

WALL

A VERY SILLY STORY BOOK

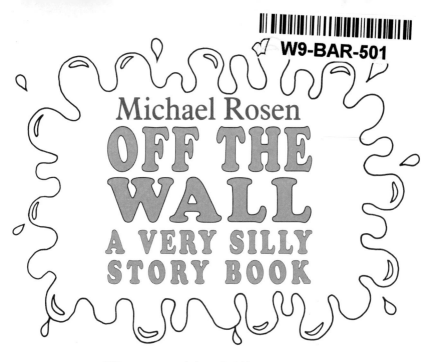

Illustrated by Mik Brown

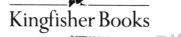

Kingfisher Books

N E W Y O R K

Contents

OFF THE WALL

A VERY SILLY STORY BOOK

KINGFISHER BOOKS
Grisewood & Dempsey Inc.
95 Madison Avenue
New York, New York 10016

First American edition 1994
2 4 6 8 10 9 7 5 3 1
Text copyright © Michael Rosen 1994
Illustrations copyright © Mik Brown 1994

Library of Congress Cataloging-in-Publication Data
Rosen, Michael
Off the wall: a very silly story book / written by
Michael Rosen: illustrated by Mik Brown. – 1st
American ed.
p.   cm.
Summary: Presents an illustrated collection of
twenty-eight humorous stories.
1. Children's stories, English. 2. Humorous stories,
English. [1. Humorous stories. 2. Short stories.]
I. Brown, Mik, ill.
II. Title
PZ7.R718670f   1994
[Fic]–dc20   93-28643   CIP   AC
ISBN 1-85697-949-0

Edited by Sian Hardy
Printed in Great Britain

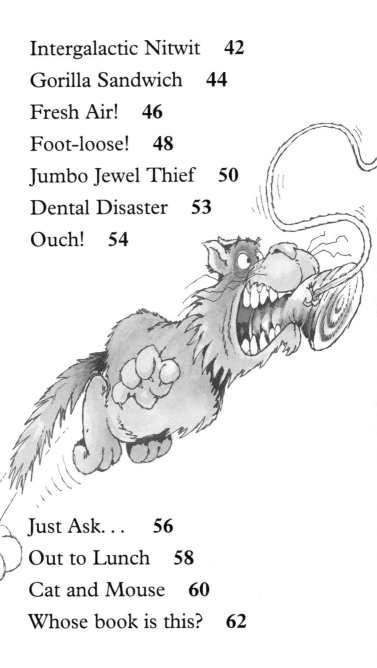

Hands Off My Hankie!

A very proper gentleman was waiting at the doctor's. Next to him was a small boy who kept sniffing.

Sniff-sniff. Sniff. SNIFF.

At last, the man couldn't stand it any more.

"Have you got a hankie?" he said.

"Yeah," said the boy, "but I ain't lending it to you."

Whee-e-e!

There were these three children and they found a magic slide. A little man was standing there and he said, "Whatever you shout when you're sliding down this slide you get as a present when you hit the bottom."

So the first kid slides down and he shouts, "GOLD!" and he lands in a great big pile of gold.

The second kid slides down and he shouts, "DIAMONDS!" and he lands in a great big pile of diamonds.

And the third kid slides down and he shouts, "WHEE-E-E! WHEE-E-E!" and he lands in a huge puddle of ...!

Thank Goodness!

There was this man, and he bought a horse, and he jumped on it and said, "GIDDYUP!" But the horse wouldn't move. So he said, "How do you make this horse go?"

And the man selling the horse said, "You say, 'Thank goodness.'"

"And how do you get it to stop?" asked the man.

And the man selling the horse said, "You say, 'Belly button.'"

So the man went off on the horse.

But the horse started going faster and faster, and the man started getting scared because he knew where the horse was taking him—right up to the edge of a huge cliff!

"Oh no," he thought, "I've forgotten how to get the horse to stop. What am I supposed to say? Oooooh, what is it?"

And the horse was getting nearer
and nearer . . .

"What's the word? Oh no . . ."
And the horse was right at the edge
. . . and he remembered.

He shouted, "BELLY BUTTON!"
And the horse stopped.

"Phew," said the man. "Thank
goodness." And the horse went
whoooosh, right over the edge.

Killer Cleaner

A boy went into a store and said, "Can I have some cleaning fluid?"

The woman in the shop said, "Do you want a cleaner to put down the toilet, one that kills germs?"

The boy said, "Yes."

So the woman said, "I've got one here that kills nearly every household germ." And she handed it to the boy.

It was in a bottle and next to it, stuck on with tape, was a great big hammer. So the boy said, "What's the hammer for?"

And the woman replied, "Well, I said that this cleaner kills nearly every household germ. The hammer is there so you can hit the last few on the head."

Double Trouble

Dave and Michael were watching a western.

As the hero, Sharpshooter Sam, rode into town, Michael said, "I bet you he falls off his horse."

Dave said, "Don't be a jerk; Sharpshooter never falls off his horse."

"I bet you he falls off his horse in this movie," said Michael.

"I bet you fifty cents he doesn't," said Dave.

They watched the movie for a little
longer. Suddenly some guns went off,
Sharpshooter's horse reared up, and
Sharpshooter fell off his horse.

"See, I told you he would," said
Michael.

"Oh, all right," said Dave. "Here's
your fifty cents."

Michael hesitated. "No, I can't
take your money," he said. "I've seen
the movie on video already."

"So have I," said Dave, "but I
didn't think he'd be stupid enough to
fall off again."

Excuses, Excuses!

There was a phone call for the principal, so she picked up the phone and said, "Yes?"

And a voice said, "I'm very sorry, but Darren Wilkins won't be at school today."

So the principal said, "Why not?"

And the voice said, "'Cuz he's sick in bed."

So the principal said, "Oh dear, what a shame, and who's speaking, please?"

And the voice said, "My dad."

Water, Water, Water!

A man was going along in the desert in Arizona when suddenly his car stopped. Nothing he could do would get it to go, so he got out and started to walk. He walked and he walked and he walked and soon he was feeling terribly, terribly thirsty. Finally he saw, coming into view, a little old shack by the side of the road. He staggered up to the door and shouted, "Water, water, water."

A man stuck his
head out of the
window and said,
"Sorry pal, I only
sell ties."
So the man walked
on. And he walked and
he walked and he walked.
By now his mouth was completely
dried up. Then, he saw another little
old shack by the side of the road. He
staggered up to the door and shouted,
"Water, water, water."

A man stuck his head out of
the window and said, "Sorry
pal, I only sell ties."

So the man walked
on.

Finally he couldn't walk any more, so he crawled. He crawled and he crawled and he crawled till, coming into view, he saw a hotel. There by the side of the road, right in the middle of the desert, was the Hotel Splendid. And it really was a splendid hotel, with a doorman standing on the steps outside.

The man crawled up to the steps and gasped, "At last! Water, water, water!"

And the doorman said, "Sorry pal, you can't come in here dressed like that, you're not wearing a tie."

Medical Marvel

A little girl fell over while she was roller-skating and hurt her hand, so she went to see the doctor.

"Do you think I'll ever be able to play the piano?" she said.

"Oh yes, dear," said the doctor kindly, "you'll be able to play the piano in just a few weeks' time."

"That's amazing," said the little girl, "because I couldn't play before."

Mousetrap

A teacher asked her class if anything funny had happened to them that week. One girl told this story:

"We have mice at home and our cat is too lazy to catch them. Yesterday my Mom was late for work because there were three mice in the kitchen.

"She ran out of the house and, on the way to the station, she rushed into a store that sells mousetraps. 'Quick, I need a trap,' she said. 'Please hurry, I have to catch a train.'

"And the man in the shop
said, 'Sorry, ma'am, we don't have
any mousetraps that big.'"

Duck!

"Mom, Mom," shouted Tom, "Little Sally's broken my toy train."

"Now that's naughty, Sally," said Mom. "How did she do it, Tom?"

"She didn't duck when I threw it at her," said Tom.

Pig!

The doctor knocked on the door of Farmer Griffiths' house. Rosie, his little girl, opened the door.

"Is your father in?" asked the doctor.

"No," said Rosie.

"Will he be back soon?" asked the doctor.

"Oh yes," said Rosie, "he's just in the pigsty, cleaning it. You'll see which one is Father—he's the one with the hat on."

Hang it Up

Two young men who wanted to look their best for going out on the town were checking out each other's clothes.

One of them said to the other, "Your coat is a mess, you should use a coat hanger."

The next week when they met, the one who had been wearing the wrinkled coat said, "I bought one of those coat hangers, but boy, they make my shoulders ache."

Mistaken Identity

There was this group of people standing around with their dogs when along came a little man with a funny-looking yellow creature on a leash.

There was another man there with a great big German Shepherd, and just for fun, he let the dog off his leash and sent it over to scare the little man and his funny-looking yellow animal.

Just as the German Shepherd came up to the funny-looking yellow animal, it lifted up its yellow head and, with one great big bite, bit the German Shepherd's head off.

The man who owned the German Shepherd said, "Oh no, what have you done? What kind of dog do you have there, anyway?"

The little man looked kind of sorry
and said, "Well, actually it's
not a dog. It's an
alligator with its
tail chopped
off. I painted
it yellow as
a joke."

Double Saving

A really stingy old penny-pincher fell into the canal. Luckily for him, a young man was walking by who dived in and pulled him out.

"Thank you very much, young man," said the miser. "You've saved my life and I would like to reward you."

He put his hand into his pocket and pulled out a ten dollar bill.

"Oh," he said, "I would have
given you five dollars, but I'm afraid
all I've got is a ten dollar bill. I'm very
sorry." And he turned to go.

"That's no problem," said the
young man. "Just jump in again and
I'll save you a second time."

Race Against Time

Mr. Smith was leaving to go to Chicago. He had four minutes to catch his train to the airport. His family was standing on the sidewalk saying goodbye to him when suddenly he realized he couldn't find his plane ticket.

So he said to his son, "Run back to the apartment and see if I left the ticket up there."

The family lived on the tenth floor ... and the elevator wasn't working. The son ran off. Three minutes later he was back, panting like he'd run a marathon.

"Yes, Dad," he said, "your ticket's on the table, right where you left it."

Can I Help You?

A man was sitting in a café having a drink when he called the waitress over. He pointed to his cup.

"This stuff tastes funny. What do you call it? Coffee or tea?"

"What do you mean, sir?" said the waitress.

"It tastes like paint," said the man.

"Oh well," said the waitress, "if it tastes like paint, it must be coffee. Our tea tastes like soap."

Pencil
Puzzle

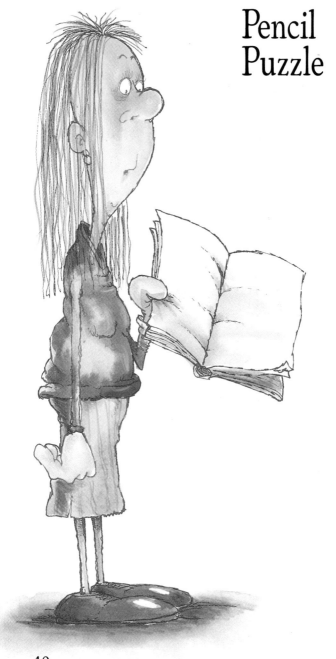

Everyone was in the classroom when the teacher said, "Where's your pencil, Maggie?"

"Ain't got one, ma'am," said Maggie.

And the teacher said, "How many times have I told you not to say, 'ain't got one'? Listen: I haven't got one. You haven't got one. They haven't got one. Now, do you understand?"

And Maggie said, "Well, where are all the pencils if nobody ain't got none?"

Intergalactic Nitwit

There was this man who wanted to become an astronaut. So he went to the Space Center and took all kinds of tests. He thought he had done really well, but the day after the tests, he got a letter telling him he had failed.

"What went wrong?" asked his friend. "What did they ask you?"

"Well, the professor asked me, 'How will you know when you've reached the Moon?' So I said, 'There'll be a great big bump, sir.'

"Then the professor asked me 'What's the first thing you should

do when you reach the Moon?'
and I said, 'Try to get back.'

"Then they told me to check the
batteries. The professor said, 'I think
they're dead.' So I said, 'Yes, they are
very dead. Why should they be alive?'

"After that we went up for a flight,
and the professor said, 'What is your
height and position?' So I replied, 'Five
foot ten, and I'm in the driver's seat.'

"And after all that, they didn't give
me the job!"

Gorilla Sandwich

A man went on vacation in Africa and bought a gorilla. On the way back he was coming through customs and he thought, "Oh no, I'm never going to be able to get through here; I know

you're not allowed to bring gorillas in. I'll have to smuggle it in."

So he slapped thick slices of bread with butter on both ears of the gorilla and walked up to the customs officer.

The customs officer went looking through all of his bags and suitcases and, when he was finally finished, he looked up and pointed at the gorilla.

"What's that?" he said.

The man got angry and said, "Look here, of course you can go through my suitcases, but what I put in my sandwiches is my business!"

Fresh Air!

A man went into a police station one day and said, "I want to complain. I've got three big brothers. We all live in one room. One of my brothers has seventeen cats. Another one has fifteen dogs. And the third one has four goats and a pig. The stink in there is terrible. I want you to do something about it."

"Well, sir," said the policeman, "does the room have any windows?"

"Sure it does," said the man.

"Well, sir," said the policeman, "I suggest you open them."

"Are you crazy?" said the man. "I'd lose all my pigeons if I did that."

Foot-loose!

Mrs. Rossiter hadn't paid the
electricity bill. She kept getting more
bills asking her to pay, but she didn't.
In the end, the electricity company
sent a man over to cut off the
electricity. Mrs. Rossiter saw him

coming and rushed off to hide behind the curtains. Her son Mike answered the door.

"Where's your mother?" said the electricity man.

"She's out," said Mike.

"Oh, really?" said the man, looking at the bottom of the curtain. "Does she always go out without her feet on?"

Jumbo Jewel Thief

A boy was coming out of school when suddenly he saw an elephant. It walked up to a jewelry store on the corner, smashed the window, and started sucking jewels up its trunk. After it had taken all the rings, gold watches, and bracelets, it turned around and headed in the direction of the zoo.

The boy, who was called Joe, ran over to the police station to tell them what he'd seen. A policeman took down everything that Joe told him and then said, "Now, son, was this an African or an Indian elephant?"

"I don't know where it came from," said Joe.

"Well, son," said the policeman, "the African elephant has big ears and the Indian elephant has small ears. What size ears did this one have?"

"I don't know, sir," said Joe. "It had a stocking over its head."

Dental Disaster

A woman went to the dentist for a check-up. The dentist had really bad eyesight.

When the dentist was finished, he said, "Thank you very much, that's all for now, Mrs. Johnson."

And the woman said, "My name's not Johnson, it's Harvey. Remember, I'm Mrs. Harvey, the one who came to see you about sore gums."

And the dentist said, "Sore gums? I'm not surprised you've got sore gums. I've just pulled out all your teeth."

Ouch!

The sixth grade class was talking about television. It was having a discussion about violence on TV.

Hui-Lin said that violence was OK, as long as there wasn't too much of it.

James thought there shouldn't be any violence at all.

Then Maria said, "I used to like television, but all the violence turned me off. Every time I changed channels, my brother hit me!"

Just Ask...

A girl was asking her dad a few things:

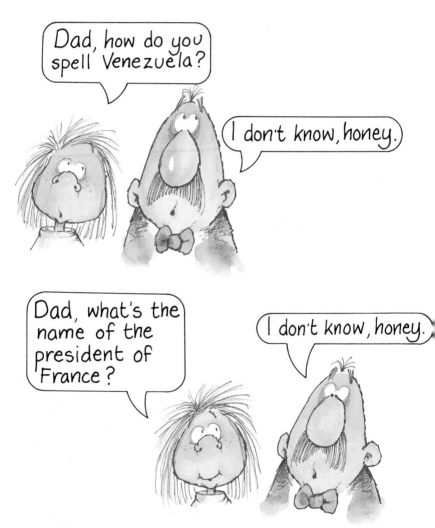

Out to Lunch

A man went to buy a car in New York City.

"Is this a good fast car?" he asked the salesman, pointing to a Super Whizzo Fast model.

"Fast?" replied the salesman. "Why, if you got in that car now, you could have your lunch in Dallas. Do you want to buy it?"

"I'll think about it," said the man, and he went home.

The next day he came back.

"I don't want that car," he told the salesman. "I was awake all night thinking about it, but I couldn't think of a single reason why I'd want to have lunch in Dallas."

Cat and Mouse

A man telephoned the doctor in a terrible state.

"Doctor, my girlfriend fell asleep in the armchair with her mouth open and a mouse ran into her mouth. What do I do?"

"Don't worry about it," said the doctor. "Just tie a chunk of cheese to a piece of string and put it in your girlfriend's mouth. When the mouse bites it, you can pull him out."

"Thank you, Doctor," said the man. "I'll run over to the supermarket

now and get a can of cat food before it shuts."

"Cat food?" said the doctor. "What do you want a can of cat food for?"

"Oh," said the man, "I forgot to tell you ... I have to get the cat out first."

Whose book is this?

Michael Rosen wrote the words and Mik Brown drew the pictures. Here are some very silly facts about them.

Michael Rosen was born. When he was young he was a boy, though now he is a man. He's been collecting jokes and silly stories for

many years. He catches them with a large net and puts them in little cages on the windowsill and under the table. His house is now full of jokes and five of them are children. They collect jokes too, but most of them are too rude to mention.

Mik Brown first started illustrating jokes when he lived on a farm. His pigs, sheep, and chickens would tell him their funniest jokes and insist on posing for drawings. Mik can illustrate almost anything but he's not wild about drawing elephants. It's not that he doesn't like them or find their jokes funny, it's just that they take up too much room on his drawing board.

**NEW YORK MILLS
PUBLIC LIBRARY**
401 Main Street
New York Mills, N.Y. 13417
(315)736-5391

MEMBER
MID-YORK LIBRARY SYSTEM
Utica, N.Y. 13502

120100